Shadow Work Journal and Workbook for Beginners

Your Companion Guide with Interactive Prompts to Integrate The Shadow, Stop Self-Sabotaging Behaviors and Unleash Infinite Creativity

Written by

Victoria Stevens

The Oath

I, _____ in the face of past adversity and painful sensory experiences lived so far, hereby pledge to resolve what troubles my soul and to recognize, accept, and nurture my wounds.

I vow to be open to guidance and to complete the pages of this journal with commitment and self-compassion, embracing both the conscious and unconscious parts of my being.

I further recognize that living in space and time, as a Creation amongst other Creations, affects my collective destiny. As I heal myself, I heal my family, my community, and I release my ancestors.

I acknowledge to be accountable for my own happiness and fulfilment. As I bring my shadow to light, I bring more light into the world. Love, Joy, Peace and Abundance will manifest as a result.

My legacy to the world is to

_____

So, Be It!

Start Date_____

Signature _____

Completion Date_____

bit.ly/3Zvkcg8

<u>YOUR FREE GIFT: GUILT and SHAME</u> <u>IN THE HEALING PROCESS OF TRAUMA AND FORGIVENESS. UNDERSTANDING THESE EMOTIONS AND HOW TO MOVE PAST THEM.</u>

Dear reader, this is a free gift to you for placing your trust in my hands and for giving me the opportunity to guide you.

I want you to understand that you are carrying great power within you, and that there are many benefits and blessings associated with you doing Shadow Work. The greatest of all are finding a sense of purpose inside you and harmony all around you.

However, it is never easy to undertake this "solo" journey and you should always allow yourself plenty of time to fully process your memories and the feelings associated with them. This includes to stop reading and journaling for a while or seek professional help should you ever feel completely overwhelmed.

To maximize the value that you are going to receive from this book, I highly encourage you to join our tight-knit community on Facebook. Here you will be able to connect and share with other like-minded- Shadow Workers in our continuing path to growth. Taking this journey alone can be tricky, so this is an excellent support network for you. It would be great to connect with you there.

Victoria Stevens

<u>>> Join Our Fb Group Self-Acceptance Through Shadow Work <<</u>

We're here
because of you

If you have found any value in this material,
Please consider leaving a review and joining the Author's
Mission to bring more healing into this world
By scanning the QR-Code below ♥

★ ★ ★ ★ ★

Contents

Introduction

With this journal workbook on **Infinite Creativity**, you will be able to experience the healing power of the psychotherapy method called Shadow Work, a well-researched method with which you can explore themes in your life that include, but are not limited to, exploring root causes of self-sabotaging behaviours, such as procrastination, lack of focus, fatigue, fear of failure, lack of inspiration, poor time-management, and social influences. Sometimes these external factors in our lives create a paralyzing conflict. It enacts reactions out of us piloted by the sense of abandonment and repressed positive qualities that are shielded by a 'shadow'.

Creativity is a fundamental part of human life. While we do not always see it as the most important skill, it contributes to our overall mental wellbeing and provides a healthy escape in everyday life. Often seen as the illogical brain function, creativity is so much more than this. We like to package the expression of self as obnoxious, a waste of time and more often than not its use is diminished, but in reality, it's a freeing experience. Society has a belief that in order to thrive, we have to block this crucial manifestation of self in favor of the typical conservative life. Excessive use of colors and the portrayal of 'abnormal behaviors' can cause a sense of being judged by others. The truth of the matter is, that creativity is extraordinarily important to the art of healthy escapisms and self-reflection. Actually, in order to be ourselves, we should express ourselves and break free from the constricted thoughts that want us to be constrained to certain behaviors.

The aim Shadow Work is to inform and empower you, adding more meaning to your life. The objective of this journal workbook is to connect theory and practice in a journey that will inform and empower you through the integration of self-expression and adding more meaning to your life. Through the application of daily affirmations, quotes, and powerful images, which will be structured across this book, you should find ample inspiration to unlock your inner creativity through the power of the self-reflection tool known as journaling.

This won't be an average journal and workbook, instead, it will focus on exploring what makes you unique and authentic, using the art of psychoanalysis to help your inner reflection and healing from suffering that might have manifested in your early years. With the added writing and interactive prompts and quotes to draw inspiration from, you will be able to go on a recorded healing journey that can be reviewed.

This will be a two-part journaling and illuminating experience that will cover some basics of Shadow Work and deliver unique affirmations to get you through the day.

This book is divided into:

- **Part One: Self-assessments and writing prompts to help you understand your Shadow.**
- **Part Two: Metamorphosis into the awareness of self and how to express that creatively and with joy.**

With the help of these two parts, your journey can start. This book is a project based on recently renewed psychotherapy methods and offers itself as a journal and workbook in your own personal self-help journey.

How the Shadow is Created

"Like a shadow, I am and I am not," - Rumi.

In a nutshell, **The Shadow** is created from childhood experiences and normally represents our darkest, hidden personality traits. It takes everything negative in our life and inherently embodies it, becoming a mirror reflection of self to our external appearance towards our everyday environments. Many people reject this part of themselves because confronting the shadow often makes people quite uncomfortable and can provide a sense of fear and apprehension in their daily lives. The shadow becomes the part of you that you refuse to acknowledge in the mirror, that tiny dose of self-loathing we tend to suppress as far as possible in our minds. Think of the shadow as your emotional punching bag.

We create the shadow subconsciously and its manifestations can become quite intentional and physical (for further explanation, see other publications on the topic). What usually happens after it's formed is that we only notice its existence in times that make us feel confined within the shackles of the mind. It usually tends to present itself in moments where we feel unfulfilled, and the trajectory of our lives causes us great unhappiness. A terrifying idea, since it seems to demand our attention. However, there is no need to panic. The shadow isn't some supernatural force that takes over you, possesses your body, and takes involuntary actions.

In this journey, it will become clear that the shadow might feel like a hated enemy who works against you. It is actually a love letter created by your mind in order to protect you from its best capabilities. While this is sometimes too protective, it's actually your friend. When you take the opportunity to 'sit' down with your shadow, you will see it has your best interests at heart. After all, it is you, and who knows you better than yourself? Jung widely believed that making your shadow a bad guy was a misrepresentation of its intentions.

While we view the shadow as a metaphorical embodiment of our worst traits, the sort of traits we 'other' from our dominant personality, it is actually a much more complex entity than that. I'd argue that what Jung intends to indicate is that the shadow is a blanket weaved in order to protect the fragile person inside. In part two, we will explore the small child hiding inside of all of us, but the basic concept is that the shadow is more of an overactive protector of our emotions. The trauma we retain throughout our adult life never really goes away, which is why the shadow manifests itself, oftentimes encouraging poor behavior in us, such as addictions or the incentive to hurt those surrounding us.

This need to hide your vulnerabilities behind a mask doesn't make you a bad person, though. There isn't a black and white with people, and though it seems blurred when the shadow is making noise, you are just a human being like the rest of us who deserves to give yourself compassion so that others can receive it too. All people are susceptible to the shadow, and what tends to happen is we see other people's shadows, that sometimes seem better or worse managed than ours, and usually we don't want to face our own because of these superficial assumptions. This is usually because as we reach adulthood, traits get sorted by society into being good or bad without any input from us.

Even things as simple as what we wear get inherently judged by society, making us feel like we are boxed in when our individual expression is robbed from us. We should all keep on striving for individualism. It's not an easy battle, but when the smoke clears, it serves to make you stronger and more confident in yourself. Maybe the lack of choice and control is what creates that aversion to the shadow since we project what society has projected on us on the shadow, the fear of losing control and being judged overpowering our need to validate and love ourselves, and not seek that validation and love solely from those around us.

We like to suppress these parts because we wish for them to go away. They won't go away, and they won't heal on their own; they leave scars, and even scabs need doctoring. The smallest of injuries can become an infection, so it needs to be treated and attended to before it kills us. Packing these issues away in the darkest parts of our minds just creates a problem for later in our lives and can cause problems that we don't always know how to face. To recap, because the shadow is created by repressing our most sensitive natures, it shows that there can be negative and positive connotations to it. It takes shape over the course of a few years and rarely shows itself in an instant when we are younger. As children, we lack the emotional maturity to acknowledge its existence. As adults, we know, because of society's expectations, that anything that reflects badly on us is to be shut away and never talked about or confronted. All these factors work together to create the shadow, and in turn, hurt us.

These prompts should help you start to get a basic understanding of the origins of your own shadow self and give you an introduction to its presence. Remember to answer these questions honestly, and don't be afraid to dive deep within yourself to unlock the past. Be caring, open-minded, and compassionate. Center yourself before answering any of these questions, as you need to be in a safe environment in order to tackle the shadow and the love you need to generate towards it and yourself.

Date:

Writing Prompts: Reflection

1. What were you like as a child?

2. What were your hopes and dreams?

3. *Who were your parents/guardians/caretakers and what were their values? How do you think their values have affected your life?*

4. What traits did they have that you hoped you didn't have?

5. *What is one thing you're afraid of because of the authority figures in your life?*

6. *Take a moment and separate traits of your parents/guardians/caretakers into two categories: Bad and good. Which ones do you resonate with the most, and how do they impact your daily life?*

7. How has this reflected upon your shadow?

8. *If you could say one thing to the shadow, what would it be?*

9. *If it's a negative feeling, how can you reiterate that into something positive and compassionate?*

10.   *If the shadow has recently given you grief, can you find a reason to forgive it?*

11.   *What would you like to be known or remembered for?*

Finish this chapter by reflecting on your answers and making a list of the most important people in your life, using one word to describe their influence on you.

The Problem with the Shadow

"Unless we do conscious work on it, the shadow is almost always projected: That is, it is neatly laid on someone or something else, so we do not have to take responsibility for it," - Robert Johnson.

Now that we understand the basis of the shadow and its creation, I think it's important to elaborate on what problems the shadow can manifest in your life. I've mentioned our relationships before and how the shadows can influence our reactions to the people in our lives. These are the unfortunate symptoms of a segregated sense of self. The goal here is to take these internal problems you might have and integrate them so you can become that masterpiece I mentioned before. The shadow can cause lots of difficulties in our everyday lives and many people call these thoughts borderline parasitical, a leech that absorbs the light into an endless hungry void. However, as Jung stated, our animosity towards the shadow is not to our benefit. Calling it a parasite is too harsh, but this comes with the innate defense mechanism towards vulnerability. Often it can feel as if we are letting ourselves get exposed, as if we stand naked in front of a crowd, and it's a big exhibit of our worst sides. A typical scenario would be when we let our insecurity about something lash out towards someone we care about, or even in our professional life.

When we struggle to come to terms with this reality, our shadow self can cause a rationalization that causes emotional pain towards others, and while the reaction isn't always invalid, it takes a mature person to realize that sometimes we act a certain way because somewhere deep down we are hurting, and an unresolved hurt can be dangerous to our personal lives. An example that can be used for this scenario is that if you experience intense verbal abuse and are subject to emotional degradation, you tend to take commentary of people very personally, meaning you are prone to impulsive decisions. If you had parents who barely gave you financial freedom, odds are that you might end up becoming addicted to spending. Oftentimes, things you lacked as a child get pushed to the extreme when you reach adulthood.

Drugs, alcohol, and other addictive substances can also become a crutch that you lean on to distract from your internal struggles. These shadow 'manifestations' of you will project itself in many ways that I'd like to go over with you so that when you do journal, it will be easy to take note of. Remember, the shadow isn't just a personality but a projection of our inner being. Projections happen when our awareness of behavior gets pushed outside of our immediate consciousness. Since our shadow is an accumulation of your rejected qualities, they become an automatic filler for your opinion on people around you. These thoughts and feelings give you an assumed perception of people. We will learn more about acceptance and integration later in the book, which will hopefully shine a light on your struggles. We want to take the negative projection and twist that to the positive projection.

How to Recognize the Shadow Within You

The symptoms of a repressed and bad shadow relationship include behavioral patterns and external projections, such as getting triggered by people and their behaviors towards us, especially when they do something that unintentionally offends us. While offending us isn't acceptable behavior, when we suppress our shadow, we deal with it in a way that is detrimental to our personal growth, implementing unhealthy patterns in our behavior. Learning internal acceptance encourages compassion towards ourselves and ultimately to outside parties.

Another symptom of the shadow self is that we also become people pleasers. We become so afraid of disappointing those around us that we hide our own truths from them and tend to say yes to requests we would rather not have agreed to. This behavior is often a throwback to our childhood and can be connected to how we were raised around our parents. For example, children who had parents that put an extensive amount of academic pressure on them can often grow up to become overachievers and develop anxiety disorders.

There are few more symptoms of a shadow self, including, but are not limited to:

- Criticizing and judging other people who do not comply with the "social norm" and act freely in the way they express themselves

- When you feel judged, or as if people are watching your every move, that normally derives from insecurity created by the shadow self.

- Emotional triggers, such as things that upset us on a deep level.

- Possible feelings of overwhelming anxiety and fear, sometimes your shadow self, create a feeling of imposter syndrome. Where you feel as if you're constantly on the verge of being "caught out."

- Emotional indifference is also a symptom of a shadow self-hiding beneath the surface. We usually take negative experiences and pack them away as a form of dealing with trauma. In turn, creating the automatic reaction to intense emotional situations with a lack of reaction, which is bad because that means we will only experience the accumulated emotions at a later, unexpected date.

Bringing the Shadow to Light

You've learned about a few results of a suppressed shadow, meaning it's time to delve into the confrontation as part of the shadow. It's a crucial step in the art of shadow work and will help you move on with your life and get a deeper understanding of the things plaguing your personal life, relationships, and work balance. But why confront and trigger your shadow, you ask? Wouldn't it be better to instead avoid the messy situation of triggering negative emotions from your early childhood? Healthy triggers aren't impossible, and in fact, should be encouraged. Only when we start unpacking the shadow and its behavior will we learn to live and let it live. It is like unclogging a pipe and having free flow again, but a pipe can't be unclogged without a plumber and a manual to the tools necessary.

The consequences of letting your shadow stay in the dark can be things such as anxiety, depression, and picking up bad habits. We do things to circumvent the void in our personal abyss, using distractions to avoid the genuine issue. All these things become crutches to feel quick moments of happiness.

How do we confront the shadow, and where do we start? It is important to center yourself before attempting any sort of triggering behavior. You want to be as comfortable and open-minded as possible to avoid major total negative regression into a headspace that encourages destructive behavior traits. You are the only one who knows your limits, and while it is important to push and challenge these limits; it is also important to acknowledge your limits and then make the decision to set a space up where you can converse and challenge our shadow's preconceived shape.

Introspection with Interactive Prompts

- Find a space, it can be your room or the living room—maybe even put on some soothing music in the background and center your mind to feel at ease with the preparation to explore your repressed psyche. It will be important to have a journaling space near you so that you can document your progress, which is an excellent tool for personal reflection later on.

- After you have created the confrontation space, it is time to approach the shadow with an open mind and full honesty. The point of triggering its reactive responses is so that you can look at those "ugly parts," or yourself, and accept them unconditionally. Take the negative bits about yourself and inspect them. Reject the input of your inner critic, open the wounds, and expose the raw parts of your psyche.

- Start asking yourself tough questions, ones that make your insides squirm—think of regrets you have or a moment in your life where the power was taken from you. Take that power back and answer the questions with total transparency.

- Naturally, through this process, you should eventually enter the phase of childhood reflection and start going over the events that have led you up to your current state, which will often be painful and create a sense of fear, and I know from personal experience, regresses you back to your most vulnerable state. It is important to give that inner child a hug and assure them they are safe here.

- In this state, you can start asking questions such as, was I completely accepted? What was expected of me? Was it realistic, and what emotional reactions were seen and judged by those around you, especially your parents?

- As you start to ask these questions and eventually transition into answering them, you will realize that these new behaviors and total courageous honesty cultivate a sense of relief in you, which leads to self-love and acceptance. As you get to know your shadow self, you realize that a lot of your behavior can be explained, and in turn, ratified. Knowing is the first step to healing. Use the pages that follow to write down any reflection that come up to your mind.

Reflections

Reflections

Reflections

The Inner Child

Now, I am going to briefly introduce you to your **inner child**: a joyful, curious part of you that builds upon wonder in your life. The child is the one that makes you braver and stronger; it helps boost your self-esteem and encourages that confidence we often lack in our lives. It is all about your inner child and who it is. If you've experienced trauma in your life, it's possible that your child is wounded, which could be why you struggle to build up that confidence and need to accept yourself fully. So, I'd say **the shadow** is normally a blanket or protective defense mechanism you have subconsciously created to fight against the fear and shame that usually surrounds the traumatic events in your life. The child is the part of you who wishes to run free.

Normally, this child comes out in moments when you do something that is often seen as childlike. When the shadow remains unresolved, we tend to package these mannerisms as shameful, hence punishing the child for just expressing itself, which is never an advisable thing to do. With the shadow there to 'protect' the inner child from negative feelings, it ends up hurting the child, often regurgitating behaviors it learned when you were a child. It becomes a metaphorical parent with what you used to express yourself in your daily life.

Letting the shadow become this protector might sound like the right idea at first, but it's actually not always a good thing since the shadow hides our inner child, meaning parts of us that used to be filled with wonder and dreams. The creative and intuitive parts of us are hidden away even more so than the shadow, ending up unintentionally stifling the joy we feel over small, good things and that can end up causing us depression and lack of motivation.

In the next few sections, we will go over how the inner child is found, and how to reach the emotional intelligence needed to become your inner child's nurturer. We want to explore the links between the **inner child**, **co-dependency**, and **toxic**

relationships formed because of how the shadow covers up the good parts of our inner child, accumulating to a greater understanding of self.

What is the Inner Child?

"Hold the hand of the child that lives in your soul. For this child, nothing is impossible," - Paulo Coelho.

When you peel back the layers and layers of the shadow, at some point you will reach the inner child; a personality archetype that is formed in the unconscious mind and holds the key to our ability to dream. In this part of ourselves, we enact, with imaginative vigor, our unmet needs. It's essentially the part of our mind where we dream and encourage imagination. There can also lie bits of a repressed childhood, especially if they did not give us the chance to really live that carefree life. Quite a few people who were forced to grow up too fast have expressed their loss at what they see as happiness because children are still naïve and can't always see the bad surrounding them. It is partly why the shadow is formed in the first place; the minds aren't yet developed to coherently understand why something has happened to them, and this becomes internalized.

It is only when they are older that it comes to light. Many parents, in fact, who take out negative feelings on their children have their shadows haunting them. Many children tend to trigger these reactions unintentionally and because the parents haven't done their internal reflection, it causes problems further down the road. It is usually common knowledge that people who bully were often bullied themselves, all part of the vicious cycle of abuse and trauma that sort of draws in the victim due to familiarity. Shadow work is great for breaking the vicious cycle and it will help bring out the inner child's ability to thrive creatively and use their institution more. It creates a strong trust within yourself (for a deeper understanding of this topic please see my other publications).

Unlocking Your Creativity Through Integration

You've gone over the hardest parts of the shadow work odyssey, like Greek hero Odysseus. It is time to return home and reclaim what was once yours. You battled the monsters, avoided the sirens, and narrowly avoided being turned into a pig by a Circe. Your child and shadow are Penelope, awaiting your return, and even though you have aged, and your appearance is different, you are still, by essence, your old self. The reunion of these two is the symbolism for when you become your full self and help push for wholeness. To reiterate, you need to make sure you follow the steps needed to encourage unification. Steps such as:

- Accepting the Past: Stifled memories that we avoid and can't be controlled need to be brought into the light despite if that makes us feel uncomfortable. When we do partake in this process, it's important to be aware of our triggers and not push ourselves so much that we lose sight of the important task. The positive note to this step is that it means when the past resurfaces in our daily lives, it's no longer so impactful in its outward and emotional force. Now we can finally grab hold of the bad thoughts, process them, and let them go. By accepting what we cannot change, we can let go and forgive for the sake of ourselves.

- Dissect your current life choices based on the past's influence: One of the most humbling experiences is realizing that other people are inherently broken, including the authority figures we were raised with. Dissecting your behavior and comparing it to others helps you understand that everyone has a shadow, and it gives that near-unconditioned compassion needed to make the right choices for ourselves and offer grace to those who hurt us. It's by no means a reason to let them back in your life since many people who are the way they are because of generational cycles won't always be able to heal. But your healing and breaking that cycle is the right move. We can't change the past, but we can change the way we perceive it.

- <u>Connecting the dots:</u> Many people suggest meditation as a way to center your mind to get it in a space that creates serenity. This you can do in many ways and is important for the convergence of self. For example, an alternative to meditation can be putting on some calm instrumental music so that your mind gets cleared and you can start to align all your thoughts into a more coherent zone. In the zone, you will be able to bridge the gap between the inner child and shadow. This harmonic connection will unlock the individualism within.

To keep up this process of authenticity, just remember to keep your journaling up to date and never lose sight of all the progress you've made. Your hard work will pay off, and even if you can't see that now, eventually, if enough time has passed, the image will become clear, and the healing will slowly start showing results.

The Basics of Creativity

"The world always seems brighter when you've just made something that wasn't there before," - Neil Gaiman.

The next part is vital to your emotional growth. I know I have said that all the other steps are important, but this is too. Truth be told, none of the steps we have gone over is any less important than the other. All these parts make up a complete story. Your story, my story—the well-being of your mind and the history of your identity. The inner child and shadow might be two separate counterparts of each other, but they can work together as a unit. Therefore, part three of the book is so important. You have the puzzle pieces organized, color-coded, and ready to be packed. The remaining question is how? How are you going to merge yourself, the shadow, and the child into a full entity? By being creative and participating in some healthy escapism. In the next few sections, I will go over what you need to do to unlock that unified force sleeping beneath the surface, and how to embrace individualism and freedom of expression beyond society's expectations. If you have heard of Friedrich

Nietzsche and his theories on the rejection of unrelated moral standards and societal values, then his story on the Camel, Lion, and Child is the perfect manner in which you can observe the full integration of oneself.

Part three is the crescendo in the symphony, the moment the build-up breaks, and the conductor sets loose a beautiful mix of noise that played together creates an unforgettable song. This is your song, and if you want to find your tune, let me take you on one more journey so that once you are ready, you can finally stand on your own, and become the assertive person you've always needed to be.

Creativity is a fundamental part of human life. While we do not always see it as the most important skill, it contributes to our overall mental wellbeing and provides a healthy escape in everyday life. Often seen as the illogical brain function, creativity is so much more than this. We like to package the expression of self as obnoxious, or as a waste of time, but in reality, it's this freeing experience and oftentimes its use is diminished. Society has a belief that in order to thrive, we have to block this crucial manifestation of self in favor of the typical cardboard life. Excessive use of colors and the portrayal of abnormal behaviors can cause this sense of judgment from other people. The truth of the matter is, that creativity is extraordinarily important to the art of healthy escapisms and self-reflection, which does not mean that working a 9-5 job is a bad thing or liking neutral colors makes you boring, that's not at all what I'm implying. I simply say that in order to be ourselves, we should express ourselves and break free from the constricted thoughts that want us to be constrained to certain behaviors. What is the expression, though? At its root, expression is making your thoughts and feelings known, and with the writing prompts, that is exactly what you have been doing. Bringing your thoughts and feelings to light, you are removing the negative power that binds it in your subconscious. I cannot express enough just how important this search for freedom is. The best part is, you don't have to be an artist to be expressive. It's in the finer details that you truly shine. Never forget that.

Being 'artistic' might be the traditional view of creativity, but it is by no means the only way you can unlock your inner self. Creativity can be expressed and expanded upon through so many varieties of hobbies, jobs, and everyday activities. Strangely enough, this also includes mathematics, a subject seen as boring by the majority of people. Matter-of-factly, mathematics was developed by dreamers and like-minded people who enjoy thinking of alternative solutions to complex problems. Math shadow work! Incredibly, something as simple as an outfit you picked out in the morning can be a way to bring therapeutic relief. Personally, I know of people who like to mismatch their socks, which gives them an extra spring in their step for the day. If you are stuck in a cubicle all day, adding personalized pictures around you, or a tiny house plant, can be that breath of fresh air away from the mental shackles that haunt you. Humans are complex. If we were simple creatures, then we wouldn't need to constantly look inside our deepest thoughts and wouldn't be subject to change as much as we are every day. The beauty of this complexity is that we are unique, and when our shadow self is integrated with the inner child, we are truly authentic and can finally break free of the shackles of suppression.

With an integrated persona, you'll soon realize just how important it is to have that authenticity in your life. The truth will set you free, and what is creative expression but the self-actualization and representation of who you are? You might finally be able to build up the confidence to set boundaries against people who only serve to create toxicity in yourself, and if you have any self-sabotaging behaviors, those will become less controlling over you because now that mindset of constant victimhood changes as you finally accept your shadow as not another, but instead as a part of yourself.

Victimhood, I hear you say, probably asking such a statement, means what? Well, let me elaborate and start by saying that in no way am I saying that any experience you have suffered over the years is directly your fault. Many times, these things happen to us and they are out of our control, which is a horrible experience, knocking us back a few steps in our life. This automatically makes us victims of circumstances, and in some ways, we will always be victims. That doesn't mean we can't reclaim our victimhood and turn it into something empowering. Negative thoughts are usually the root cause of the paralyzing effect victimhood can have on us, and it can stunt your growth as a person, which in turn pushes you right back into the darkness. As you can remember, one of the risks of shadow work is that a trigger can be too intense for you to process all at once, which is why you should have a professional constantly advising you and observing your progress so that when they see you're spiraling, you've got an anchor keeping you grounded. The best way to combat those thoughts that revert you to a victim state is to reaffirm them with positive thoughts. For example:

- I am inadequate—I am enough

- I am pathetic—I am strong

- I lack kindness—I am compassionate

- I am hated—I am loved.

These are just a few examples of how you can train your mind to think beneficially to feel assured by yourself that you are good enough. Another tip I find useful is that you can take this exercise and branch out with it, by answering why, after you've added the positive thought over the combating negative.

For example: I am loved because; my friend gives me little treats to say thank you sometimes, which gives me warmth and peace for the rest of my day.

You can even use this as a continuous writing exercise.

We all want love and the feeling of belonging, and by finding that niche, pulls us into our happy space, allowing us to find a loving community alongside it. I haven't spoken about reinvention and community yet, but I thought that before we speak about expanding upon your own personal creativity, it would be an excellent opportunity for me to broach the subject around a support system and joining and building a great community that can act as your outward positive environment. As a disclaimer, however, I want to add that there are pros and cons to joining a community of your choice, but I feel like it is one of those cases where the pros outweigh the cons. You need social interactions, and with the internet, your possibilities are endless, depending on your interest. It is filled with social media sites that encourage you to belong. From photography, poetry writing, or even blogging, the world naturally becomes your oyster and you the pearl. By surrounding yourself with people who share an interest in your hobbies and ways of relieving stress, you will be creating a temporary safe space of expression for yourself with others. Sharing and talking about these hobbies will lighten up your mind and heart, giving you that lost sense of belonging. It's a fantastic way to get to know people and practice your self-reflection.

This project and journaling steps are there to encourage belonging. You will see at the end of your journey how much growth has happened for you. It is good to gain perspective now and then. The best part is that now there is an open stage for you to not only contribute inwardly but also outwardly, and through self-acceptance, you can finally accept others.

What is your Niche and How to Combat Victimhood?

How can you contribute to your creative expression and freedom of self? In this next part, I want you to reflect upon what activity of expression gives you the best feeling of joy and freedom, but also how you can escape the choking negative thoughts that continuously put you in a bad mental space by using your own affirmative contributions to your own self.

Writing Prompts: What is Your Niche and How to Combat Victimhood

Affirmation: I am unique and my best self when I let go to express who I am.

Date:

1. *You feel the most energized when...and why?*

2. You are happiest when you...and why?

3. You feel most creative when...and why?

4. *You feel like your higher purpose could be...*

5. You feel your most comfortable in clothes that...

6. Your favorite color is... and what you relate it to?

7. The people who represent love in your life are...

8. You feel most heard when...

9. Your favorite form of affection is...

10.   *Nature represents...*

11.   *Your home is your...*

12.   *Your best version is...*

Your Destiny is Your Own!

Expanding on Your Inner Creativity

"There is no doubt that creativity is the most important human resource of all. Without creativity, there would be no progress, and we would be forever repeating the same patterns,"- Edward de Bono.

When we are creative and we use our minds to go into that space, it can make us incredibly vulnerable, which is a good thing because the space you create in your own mode of creative expression is safe. You need that space to let loose and be yourself, which is an invaluable asset in your everyday life. It takes immense energy to pack away parts of yourself that might cause sachem. Compartmentalizing our disowned sides causes that restraint from fully living in the now and perpetuates crippling fear. There is a scene we are all quite familiar with, which is the moment an artist takes the paint, scooping it up haphazardly with brushes and splatters it with all their might across a blank canvas, or even an image they had already created. It's that sense of unadulterated feeling, where you can do no wrong because you are just taking it out on the blank canvas, forming it, and shaping it into something unique, organic, and frighteningly beautiful. I talk from experience, it's an exercise to try. Get some paints and a canvas or a piece of paper and just have at it. Use the colors you are immediately drawn to and make that jumbled-up picture because, in the end, it's you. Completely you. Not a reflection of a mirror staring back at you, manipulated with light, but a colorful splatter of you. You can take that abstract piece and hang it somewhere or paint it clean again and reuse it when you need to vent out that energy.

Another reason this moment can happen is when the artist already had a picture there, almost always a symbolic sign that the picture they have crafted for themselves didn't make them happy anymore. As compared to your subconscious mind, you picked up this book because you weren't happy with your picture. You needed to be taught to repaint and reassess it again, even if it is just a steppingstone in your overall adventure. You see, creativity or an accompanying hobby is what makes us human. We can have the numbers and rationality live our lives and use these "life lessons" to escape people's ire, but that doesn't guarantee us happiness, and the world loves to sell the idea of happiness to us in a perfectly commercialized package. From the fast-food adverts to the classy alcohol lifestyles, we are constantly supposed to accept this external pressure to be joyful. True happiness comes from knowing you were true to yourself, despite what you were surrounded by.

But how do you expand on your creativity and unlock the inner potential that nests there? What are the key steps to take? One step is integration between the child and the shadow. I touched on this briefly, but I thought I'd give a quick overview of this very important step in the next paragraph.

So, as we now know, each of us carries a shadow, and that shadow reflects inadequacy, shame, and guilt; things we gained from negative experiences in our early stages of life. It is coupled with the repression of things such as sexuality, fear, and bad thoughts, but we have moved on from that thought process and have learned that the shadow is our friend who needs love, just like us. I thought I'd take the opportunity to use expression and artistic wiles to unlock the good and bad thoughts and turn them into brilliant and free abstract thoughts. You've heard of Friedrich Nietzsche, the famous nihilist that everyone liked to follow. Well, he too ascribed to a similar theory of self-actualization, and if you follow each step correctly, you'd eventually reach the inner child and become fully actualized.

"We are like shop windows in which we ourselves are constantly arranging, concealing, or illuminating our supposed qualities, which others ascribe to us—all in order to deceive ourselves," - Frederick Nietzche.

In his book, *Thus Spoke Zarathustra*, Nietzsche describes a three-part metamorphosis we must all go through to reach that enlightenment.

The Camel, which is the 'spirit' that carries the heaviest of burdens describes those who are strong enough to take the steps into self-actualization, but can oftentimes get stuck in that stage of metamorphosis. I see this as the equivalent of the shadow's relationship with you as a person. Many times, we get stuck in the confrontation stage, where instead of sealing our wounds and moving on, we make them increasingly worse (Gambardella, 2020).

"There are many things for the spirit, for the strong heavy spirit in which dwell respect and awe: Its strength longs for the heavy, for the heaviest [...] thus it kneels like the camel and wants to be well-laden,"

- Friedrich Nietzche.

These words reflect how the Camel acts, while the metaphor might sound strange as it explains the early phases of gaining new knowledge. We're not perfect, us humans, but it represents that thirst to learn and to store away all we have absorbed. Because we are strong as the Camel, we start burdening it with information and knowledge. We want to make sure we have enough of it all to survive the anguish and turmoil threatening to burst from our chests. We do things like reading, writing, traveling, and uncover the latest trinket in our lives. And the weight of all this knowledge weighs heavier and heavier, eventually, much to our dismay, we realize that we are still exactly where we were before because what is information if we don't use and adapt to it? Burnout is real, and it is dangerous because it can easily draw you back to the dark place, even if the dark place is just a terrified version of yourself.

The Lion is the second phase of the metamorphosis. The Camel, when unchanged, risks the chance of becoming bitter, lonely, and filled with despair. It doesn't help to have all the information and no way to expel that—this is where the Lion makes its appearance. "King of the Beasts," the Lion establishes its law over the land. When the Camel ventures out of the comfort of its space and heads off into the desert, which, according to Nietzsche, is humanity's expectation of the person you are, it's at this moment that the Lion truly realizes there is no limit to who you can be. In a place where everything is permitted, what are the things holding you back? The "God is Dead" theory is often misrepresented here when it is just stating that there is no higher power dictating your decisions, and instead it is entirely up to you and your own free will (Raynor, 2016).

"God is dead. God remains dead. And we have killed him, - Fredrich Nietzsche.

This is where the connection to victimhood really ties in. It sounds unfortunate, but the Lion proves that your only limit is yourself. We spend many years thinking we are chained to societal pressures that torment us, but the truth is, you were always free. It's in the desert of the human condition where the Lion boldly exclaims, "I will," a stark contrast to the Dragon, the image of societal norms, who states quite boldly, "Thou Shalt." It's a form of rejecting permission and becoming a non-conforming entity of the moral laws and societal values that try to force us into a box. You are an organic shape, to be molded by your individualism, not to be forced into a shape you never were. These are the basic thoughts behind self-expression and acceptance. It's how you start to integrate your pieces. You are the masterpiece.

Finally, there is the child. You have fought hard to be the strongest, the freest, now it's time to settle down and begin anew. The child signifies your rebirth, a new beginning (for further work on the 'inner child' see book number two of this series). While the Lion exemplified "NO," the child affirms life with an astounding "YES." By rejecting all that came before, your shape is new and ready to rebuild from the ground up. You can become someone entirely new with the same essence. That's what this is all about: Your own personal essence. Who you are when no one is looking and hopefully through this process, you realize you are an extraordinarily complex and unique person who deserves love, compassion, and kindness.

"For the sport of creation: The spirit now wills its own will, ... its own world," - Friedrich Nietzche.

Your destiny is your own.

This might seem like it's a tangent away from creative expression, but this ties in quite nicely with my original points. I'd argue that Nietzsche was never a nihilist, as he has been famously miscast, but someone who grew tired of the bonds of society and its expectations on the way to act. They will try at everything to wring individualism out of you. Being different is bad. Being different is awkward. Let me let you in on a secret. We are all human at our core with genuine acceptance. True individualism is when you embrace every single flaw, weird quirk, and even bad behavior you have picked up over the years, move on, grow, and let go. Therefore, creative expression is so crucial. I thought I would leave a few options for you to pick from, a way to branch out your individualism to not only yourself but to the world.

Express your Self

Creative Prompts: Express Yourself

Affirmation: "I think, therefore I am," - Rene Descartes.

Interactive Prompts to Boost Creativity

1. Take a look at the story of the Camel, Lion, and Child, and make a visual interpretation of the journey these three characters had to take to actualize their true selves. Attribute yourself to this journey. You can use anything from photography to painting. Even taking something as simple as play-doh to make a sculpture can be a good design. Record this in your workbook as a reference for later.

2. Another idea that could be fun and reflective is to draw, paint, or write in the dark. It's a good way to get an idea of how it feels to be a shadow suppressed and not in the light. After you've done this, turn on the light and start turning your creation into something subjectively beautiful. Add an animal or flower that brings significance to your life and applies to the concept of rebirth.

3. Create a collage of images that draws your attention, don't focus too much on what they are and what they represent yet. Just let them draw your attention. You can use Pinterest to make a Pinboard if you don't have access to physical materials, making what we refer to as a mood board. After you have selected a few pictures that genuinely speak to you, take a moment to study them, write what they mean to you, and how that ties in with your journey.

4. Watch a movie from your childhood that you loved and write about how it has influenced you.

5. Keep a dream journal. This suggestion might seem a bit cliche, but many artists have had their best ideas and reflective moments over dreams. They aren't some deeply spiritual experiences, your dreams are usually tied to your subconscious, so it is the perfect way to keep track of what you are going through.

6. Make a sculpture of your hand in plaster and write all the wonderful qualities about yourself on it. As a way to imply that you're the master of your destiny and destination.

7. Remember to have fun and join a community. If you enjoy reading, join a book club. If you enjoy painting, join a hobbyist paint group. There are a few people who enjoy the calming qualities of nature. It's a space where you can feel at ease away from the noise.

8. Write the negative three words you associate with yourself and then write their opposites down next to it. How does it make you feel?

9. Expressing what hobbies give you the best freedom to be yourself and do something as an example. For example, write a poem, do a collage/mood board, draw or take a picture of your favorite outfit.

10. Take the above prompt and write your thought process around why you chose that specific form of expression.

11. Come up with your own personalized affirmation/s.

12. After you've done that, take your affirmation and go do something fun with it. Maybe embroider it on a pillow? Make it something visible to you most of the time.

Letter to the Future

Letter to the Future Self

Using your newfound creative inspiration, write a letter to yourself 10 years into the future. Really note down where you want to be emotionally, physically, and in your career path. Take a moment to visualize where you want to be in the next few years, create that space to live in and to experience, then write the letter with all that in mind. Thank your future self for getting this far, for being willing to go through all the heartache and hurt in order to thrive to their better selves. Acknowledge the struggles they might have come across and the relationships that had to change. Like with the child, reassure them that all of this is a temporary stop and that you are sure they ended up doing the right things for themselves. Maybe even tell them how excited you are that you can finally take the steps to your progression, and that you're excited to see your story unfold. Be bold, be brave, and always be authentic to who you are. When you find yourself reading the letter again, you will have the perfect story to treasure as you walk into your life with a lighter, informed step. This is your narrative that you have created, and this letter, as well as those before, prove that it's all in your control now, no one else can have the power over you again. With this final letter, I know you will become empowered.

Date:

Writing Prompts: Letter to the Future

Writing Prompts: Letter to the Future

Writing Prompts: Letter to the Future

Writing Prompts: Letter to the Future

Writing Prompts: Letter to the Future

"What we call the beginning is often the end. And to make an end is to make a beginning. The end is where we start from,"
– T.S Elliot.

Conclusion

I'll admit, ending this book is quite difficult for me, and I'm sure, in a way, now that its pages are filled with your soul, you too feel that loss. The good news is, while I am moving on, you still have a complete story to tell, and this is hardly the end. It's your beginning. We have cried, we have laughed, and we have grieved. Take courage, there is a beauty beyond your pain, and like the phoenix, you will rise from the ashes and be born anew. You are an independent, strong, and wonderful person who has been shaped by negative experiences and no longer controlled. You are not alone. This book is a personal project for many, and just because my words end at the end of the book, your words will live on in more journals and more artistic endeavors. I know that while you have suffered, there's renewed hope that your light was never lost and has always been there. Share it. It is a shame to hide someone as incredible as you in an isolated instance.

They always say goodbyes are the hardest. Personally, I think it's the strength to continue fighting and living that is the hardest part. A goodbye is final. The fight is ongoing, but even that will come to its end one day. I'll leave you with this: Be the best you. Don't let anyone define who you are and who you are going to be. Be assertive in who you are and let yourself make mistakes, encouraging grace to yourself because you can only learn from those mistakes. Give yourself a break now and then, don't let the guilt control you. Some days we need a lazy day in order to reset ourselves. Every day doesn't have to be about work, relationships, and self-improvement. Self-love is also knowing when all you need is to curl up in your bed and sleep like the dead. Do you enjoy reading? Do that. Video games? No problem. Escapism is good for you. Draw and write those stories, find your love language, whatever you need, it's ok to be just a bit selfish sometimes. I'm not saying hide forever, but grant yourself the privilege of a moment's rest, the world will still be there when you come back. It's not going anywhere. Not yet anyway.

I hope this has been enlightening, and I hope that you have found the peace within yourself to move to greater and better things. You are loved. Good luck.

Extra Resources

I hope you have enjoyed your journey so far. If you would like to continue your journey to self-discovery even further, you should consider looking at these extra resources of mine:

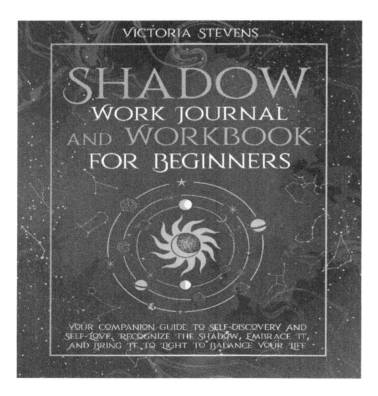

This interactive journal with exercises, worksheets, and prompts will take your self-discovery journey a step further. It will help you reflect on your life and your relationships, and it will help you solve your internal struggles by increasing self-awareness, self-compassion, and self-love.

To Your feeling of Wholeness!

What is next? Well, if you feel like going even further on your path to self-discovery and liberation, you should continue with this other resource of mine:

With this Journal Workbook you will learn how to set healthy boundaries by overcoming the emotional triggers of trauma bonding and generational trauma. The focus will be on increasing awarness about what has happened to you during your upbringing and discover if your inner child is wounded with guiding prompts for inner child healing and growth. It will also offer you a section on re-parenting the inner child so that you can be that soothing parent that you might have missed in crucial moments of your life. The aim of this work is to let you rediscover the most <u>joyful, witty and playful</u> part of your Self so you can let it emerge and come out to the forefront of your personality so that you can live life from a place of joy.

To Your Happiness!

Please note, each Journal Workbook has its own internal coherence and aim. However, the topics are intertwined and are all based on the same psychotherapeutic principles therefore you might encounter repetitions of concepts such as the Shadow and Inner Child while the writing prompts are mostly different. To be honest though, most of my clients still benefit from revising the same ideas from time to time, because while you are developing your consciousness certain concepts can change meaning and become clearer with time. It is also important to keep tracing your changes in understanding and taking notes of them.

Author Bio

Victoria Stevens is the author of several Self-Help books.

Victoria's interest in childhood trauma and development began very early in her life. Since childhood she was verbally and emotionally abused by her highly manipulative and authoritarian parents, which brought her enormous suffering.

Victoria found herself approaching life disheartened because of her parents' effect on her self-confidence and self-love and found herself living several stories and friendships, one more troubled than the other!

To the young Victoria the world felt a very unpredictable and unsafe place, but not being the kind of woman who gives up easily, Victoria decided to delve into the theories of developmental psychology and childhood trauma to try and alleviate the suffering she sees in herself and so many people.

Victoria has already helped thousands of people regain a healthy and successful self-image, healing their inner child, integrating all their inner parts living in the shadow, and achieve a sense of wholeness and freedom. Her daily practice has been heavily influenced by the scholarship of Carl Jung and many other well-renewed psychologists, psychotherapists, and physicians.

The author's mission is to share with as many people as possible her most effective methods for resolving inner issues through the famous method of "shadow work journaling workbook with prompts" and the "3 letters to Improve personal awareness and authenticity". These concepts represent her greatest discoveries and her most successful tools in counselling her clients.

Victoria herself is also a nature enthusiast and loves to journal to feel connected to the world outside. She didn't grow up religious and wanted to find a way to bypass the usual religious idea behind self-improvement and healing. She wants to express that there are many alternatives to your journey that don't require meditation or religion. She wants this book to be something different and to reassess the fideistic approach to healing.

This is where her love for journaling and nature comes in handy as she uses these moments to record her thoughts and feelings. Always writing and reflecting on the moments in her life and wondering about where she is going. Victoria is a big enthusiast of analytical psychology and wants to use what she has learned to inspire others and most importantly, herself. Using the skills and research she has accumulated; she wants to make the most of her values and advance in her career as writer.

She knows that through deeper connections, everybody can lead a meaningful life. She strongly suggests the art of Shadow Work to work through insecurities such as past failures, loss, and grief. The use of these techniques can prevent them from spreading over to other people. When she is not at work, the author likes to spend time by the sea as it's her favorite place. From the serenity of the beach, where people can socialize and be joyful, to the unpredictable exciting ocean, life can often surprise you in the beauty it holds. It is no wonder that Victoria Stevens owns a sailboat, which she regularly takes out along the San Francisco Bay, where she can feel most at peace and in tune with herself.

Through this book, she hopes you can see her heart and vision beyond the ordinary and let it take you on a journey of growth and love. Fighting your insecurities along the way with her, and she knows you will get a life-changing experience from her books.

We're here because of you

If you have found any value in this material,
Please consider leaving a review and joining the Author's
Mission to bring more healing into this world
By scanning the QR-Code below ♥

★ ★ ★ ★ ★

References

Arabi, S. (2018, June 6). What Is The Shadow Self? And How Do I Do Shadow Work? Thought Catalog. https://thoughtcatalog.com/shahida-arabi/2018/06/shadow-self-shadow-work/

Capacchione, L. (1991). Recovery of your Inner Child: The highly acclaimed method for liberating your inner self. (Illustrated). Touchstone. https://www.amazon.com/Recovery-Your-Inner-Child-Liberating/dp/0671701355

Centre of Excellence. (2019, September 16). What is Shadow Work? Centre of Excellence. https://www.centreofexcellence.com/what-is-shadow-work/

Emma. (2021, June 3). 33 Journal Prompts From a Seasoned Shadow Worker. Medium. https://medium.com/mystic-minds/33-journal-prompts-from-a-seasoned-shadow-worker-fc74ab962505

Ford, D. (2001). The Dark Side of the Light Chasers: Reclaiming your power, creativity, brilliance, and dreams. Hodder & Stoughton.

Fordham, F., & Michael S.M. Fordham. (2019). Carl Jung | Biography, Theory, & Facts. In Encyclopædia Britannica. https://www.britannica.com/biography/Carl-Jung

Fosu, K. (2020, December 14). Shadow Work: A Simple Guide to Transcending The Darker Aspects of The Self. Medium. https://medium.com/big-self-society/shadow-work-a-simple-guide-to-transcending-the-darker-aspects-of-the-self-e948ee285723

Gambardella, S. (2020, August 21). Nietzsche's three steps to a meaningful life. Medium. https://medium.com/the-sophist/nietzsches-three-steps-to-a-meaningful-life-f063793adfc4

Hall, M. P. (1980). Studies in character analysis: phrenology, palmistry, physiognomy, graphology, Oriental character analysis. Philosophical Research Society.

Inner Shadow Work Website. (2021, March 17). 30+ Powerful Affirmations for Shadow Work. https://innershadowwork.com/affirmations-for-shadow-work/

Jeffrey, S. (2019, April 15). Shadow Work: A Complete Guide to Getting to Know Your Darker Half. Osage. https://scottjeffrey.com/shadow-work/

Jung personality test. (2019). 123test.com. https://www.123test.com/jung-personality-test/

Liang, L. (2019, March 30). Three Metamorphoses: Camel, Lion, Child. Medium. https://counterreality.medium.com/three-metamorphoses-camel-lion-child-a0a184e15a06#:~:text=In%20Nietzsche

Martin Evan Jay. (2018). Sigmund Freud | Austrian psychoanalyst. In Encyclopædia Britannica. https://www.britannica.com/biography/Sigmund-Freud

Masterclass Staff. (2020, November 8). Writing 101: The 12 Literary Archetypes. Masterclass. https://www.masterclass.com/articles/writing-101-the-12-literary-archetypes#whats-the-difference-between-archetypes-stereotypes-stock-characters-and-clichs

Mcleod, S. (2018, May 21). Carl Jung | Simply Psychology. Simplypsychology.org. https://www.simplypsychology.org/carl-jung.html

Neill, C. (2018, April 21). Understanding Personality: The 12 Jungian... Moving People to Action; Conor Neill. https://conorneill.com/2018/04/21/understanding-personality-the-12-jungian-archetypes/

Owings, S. (2020, April 4). The 12 Literary Archetypes. Medium. https://medium.com/the-brave-writer/the-12-literary-archetypes-1e623ac06ca5

Paler, J. (2019, January 18). Shadow work: 8 steps to heal the wounded self. Hack Spirit. https://hackspirit.com/7-shadow-work-techniques-to-heal-the-wounded-self/

Parent Co. (2017, November 7). How a Parent's Affection Shapes a Child's Happiness for Life. The Gottman Institute; https://www.gottman.com/blog/how-a-parents-affection-shapes-a-childs-happiness-for-life/

Perry, C. (2015). The Shadow | Society of Analytical Psychology. Society of Analytical Psychology. https://www.thesap.org.uk/resources/articles-on-jungian-psychology-2/about-analysis-and-therapy/the-shadow/

Raynor, T. (2016, April 13). Nietzsche's Three metamorphoses. WordPress; Philosophy for Change. https://philosophyforchange.wordpress.com/2010/02/12/nietzsches-three-metamorphoses/

Regan, S. (2020, December 22). Meet Your "Shadow Self": What It Is When It Forms & How To Work With It. MBG Mindfulness. https://www.mindbodygreen.com/articles/what-is-shadow-work

Rosenberg, J. (2019). 90 Seconds To A Life You Love: How To Master Your Difficult Feelings To Cultivate Lasting Confidence, Resilience, And Authenticity. Little Brown Spark.

Russell, T. (n.d.). How to Get In Touch with Your Dark Side Through Shadow Work. Shape. Retrieved July 6, 2021, from https://www.shape.com/lifestyle/mind-and-body/mental-health/what-is-shadow-work

Schwartz, S. (2020, January 23). How a Parent's Affection Shapes a Child's Happiness | SPSP. Www.spsp.org. https://www.spsp.org/news-center/blog/schwartz-parents-children-affection

Seeking Serotonin. (2021, January 11). 31 Days of Shadow Work Journal Prompts For Healing and Growth. https://seekingserotonin.com/shadow-work-journal-prompts/

Sprankles, J. (2020, August 17). What Is Shadow Work? Scary Mommy. https://www.scarymommy.com/shadow-work/

Stein, C. (2019, February 14). 365 Creative Writing Prompts. ThinkWritten. https://thinkwritten.com/365-creative-writing-prompts/

All Images are sourced from Pixabay and Unsplash